WHAT DANTE DID WITH LOSS

WHAT DANTE DID WITH LOSS

JAN CONN

For Ann & Gary

Thinking of you in Illinois,
hoping you have a glorious,
happy 1995 – and that I see
you this year.

much love,
Jan.
Burlington. VT
Jan. 25/95

SIGNAL
EDITIONS

SIGNAL EDITIONS IS AN IMPRINT OF VEHICULE PRESS MONTREAL CANADA

Some of these poems have appeared in *Arc Magazine, The Antigonish Review, Event, The Malahat Review, Matrix, Prairie Fire, Prism International, Quarry, Room of One's Own, The University of Windsor Review* and *The Signal Anthology* (ed. Michael Harris, Vehicule Press, 1993). Others have been broadcast on KGNU Radio, Boulder, Colorado.

The author thanks The Canada Council for a grant to travel in Bolivia, Chile and Venezuela during 1990 when some of these poems were written.

Roo Borson, David Conn, Mary di Michele, Kim Maltman, Jane Munro, Susan Wineriter, and Michael Harris generously offered critical comments and editorial suggestions.

Published with the assistance of The Canada Council.

Signal Editions editor: Michael Harris
Cover design by Mark Garland
Photograph of the author by Page Ogden-Bruton
Typeset in Perpetua by Simon Garamond
Printed by Hignell Printing Ltd.

CANADIAN CATALOGUING IN PUBLICATION DATA

Conn, Jan, 1952-
  What Dante did with loss

Poems.
ISBN 1-55065-052-1

  I. Title

PS8555.O543P37 1994   C8811'.54   C94-900137-6
PR9199.3.C66P37 1994

Published by Véhicule Press, P.O.B. 125, Place du Parc Station, Montreal, Quebec H2W 2M9.
Distributed by General Distribution Services, Don Mills, Ontario and Niagara Falls, N.Y.

Printed on acid-free paper.

"I am leaving the hospital, thinking of the woman Poe
almost married, and if he had, there wouldn't be that story
of the child bride, eight years old when Edgar
fell in love with her, same age as Dante's Beatrice.
Paradise is what Dante did with loss. But try
to imagine what it would be like to break
bad news to Poe, stare him straight in the eyes

and say, Listen, it's over, *fini*, ended, as far
as you're concerned, she's dead, you
understand, dead. I'd rather take out the hospital garbage,
or breathe ether, handerkerchief pressed
to my face, swilling big gulps
of forgetfulness, swinging me darker
with the gulls that swim among skyscrapers, slashes of black—"

—Susan Mitchell

Contents

BEYOND LAS NIEVES

LOVE AS A MOVING OBJECT

Trop de Vert

"Apagada la luz de la poesía, por efecto de una nube cargada de ministros. Todos se queman en el mismo reverbero, se acabó la edad de la inocencia, sólo quedan peces lentos y solitarios, un diente de aviador y tres cronistas literarios. Estos escriben al viento."

—Cristina Peri Rossi

TROP DE VERT

I am writing all this down—sheared asphalt,
groves of mango and saman,
two white crosses moored by the highway,
side-by-side, ripe with symbolism,
but someone else's.

Also noting the names freshly painted in black
and the crimson and amber flowers spilling
over ochre-coloured earth.

In memory.

As we descend behind an orange-tarped truck,
surrounded by exuberant, ravenous greens.

A bust of the virgin, painted vivid blue and yellow,
looking startled,
emerges from a chartreuse wall over a doorway.

A doorway bordered entirely with minute hand-carved stars.

Fits in nicely with the two crosses,
thinks the cortex.

Trop de vert, demasiado!
insist the interneuron connections.

While the living flames of poinsettia,
unbearably bright, burn a hole
in the middle of my forehead.

ANGELS, WIND-SURFING

Late one evening in Rio—after not sleeping
for 48 hours—we ate dinner in a green
hexagonal restaurant
overlooking the dark, mercurial waves
of Guanabara Bay.

We had just come from a movie
where young male prostitutes lived together
like vagabonds in a derelict hotel

and then we had passed little enclaves
of transvestites, camping it up
in exotic costumes made for carnival

and street vendors who sold designer oranges
and live blue crabs tied together with string.

Maybe it was the lack of sleep
or the half-moon dangling from one corner
of an unrecognizable southern constellation—

we took the ferry across the bay to Niterói,
and there were dark blue angels wind-surfing
in the hallucinogenic ripples and deep swells of the waves—

their magnificent white wings catching the night wind,
their deep-set eyes joyous, and magical
and breath-taking...

LA VIRGEN DE LA PAZ

Through her clear glass eyes,
30 metres high, all the surrounding greens
somehow focused in her eyes,
I'm peering out at the *Cordillera*,
expecting, who knows, just one
parting of the clouds, some minor miracle.

Bee-bullets of black and yellow adrenaline
mainline it for the comb
hidden up in the crevasse
below the right breast. Near the dove.

What if all that energy curled up into a black
pulsating ball had nowhere to go?

And no lines on the palm of the hand,
outstretched, opening...
No future, only the bright protoplasm of the present,
pulled like a membrane,
like a polarizing filter,
over all of western Venezuela.

Look! Down there, near the mouth of
La Cueva de los Pentitentes.
A patch of flattened grass, as though
someone leaped from the eyes
and landed rolling, tumbling—
fracturing both legs, cracking the rib cage...

I know someone who did that.
I know her.

Here is her house, do you see the bedroom
is a little cage, inside the cage she perches,
singing and singing...

And look, there's a sacred corner, where she brings
flowers, a pink satin fan. A candle, the colour
of moonlight. Fossils of ferns and the delicate
tracings of leaf skeletons. And a white ceramic
bowl, with an aquamarine interior—
in which she might calmly bathe
on the hottest days.

THE PELICAN

At the end of a pitted gravel road
was a small resort where foreigners gathered
and a madwoman with blistering blue-green eyes
and bleached hair who sidled up to everyone
crooning love songs from the 50's.

Creating black umbrellas of shade,
the palms glittered with a life of their own
and people cut their feet on the broken glass and garbage
and no one went swimming

and that was the day the pelican came
up onto the sand from the murky grey water
where it perched on a bleached wooden boat
preening, giving us its profile—
dark green pouch, yellow curved tip
at the end of its beak,
unreadable blue-grey eye.

A gang of children tormented it—
poking it with sticks, trying to pull out some feathers—
and then one of the tourists who'd been drunk and abusive
the previous night
tried to feed it a frozen fish
which it tore up into strips thin as palm leaves
and stuffed inside its pouch,

which gathered something
of the burnt orange sunset into it
and something also of the woman's strangeness,
her crippled epileptic son who slept on the stairs,
her reddened lips opening and closing
like elastic bands.

THE LONG BLUE SHADOW OF CESARE PAVESE

Blue-grey houses on stilts
wade with the birds.

Behind the ash-white of the dunes,
the pale green Gulf of Mexico
pulses and breathes. Last night

on the surf, the tarnished silver light
of the quarter moon. Great clouds bearing

down. No purple phosphorescence
to make the foam light up
like a tropical forest
full of fire-flies. Today I wake

flat and ribless and frail
as a sand-dollar. Touch me,
I'll crack. You were too sad, Cesare Pavese,
to live anywhere.

How to continue to live,
chipped and cracked

like the shells—pale yellow, buff,
mottled grey, rose—

scattered on the sand
beneath the long blue shadows of sea oats

among the pines and sago palms,
blue-grey houses on stilts, wading
with the birds.

AFTER READING CHARLES DICKENS' BIOGRAPHY
BY PETER ACKROYD IN SOUTHERN FLORIDA

A woman in a white turban
asleep in one small bedroom.

A landscape of palms & hibiscus
envelops a miniature house.
The walls weighed down with trivets—
garish, metal—somehow embodying
all of southern Florida's bad taste.

Peter Ackroyd and I are taking a shower;
we agree to exchange bodies
for awhile. I slip into his
through an eardrum, down the Eustachian tube,
expanding into his lungs.

Meanwhile, he has become the size of a water molecule,
and enters me,
like a jumping jack,
down my throat when I sneeze.

An errant cloud of white egrets—so common—
obscures one of the windows,
then settles among the bright pink hibiscus.

A man (the companion of the sleeping woman?)
tries out a heavy vacuum cleaner in the cramped living room
and finds he must work around the large dog
sprawled there.

Peter and I sit quietly talking
in a limestone cave
beneath the house.

Enter Charles Dickens (into the humid dark).
A small green gecko on one shoulder.
Peter speaks to me in a low frantic voice, wanting
back his body.
No way, I say, laughing aloud,
and stand to shake hands with Mr. Dickens.

AT 7 AM THE RIVER

for Gina Aeschbacher

At 7 am the river is black and flecked with gold,
one long curving rush
over boulders stretching
like big cats
out of and into the current.

Enviously I watch the effortless movement
of billions of molecules of water,
trying to hear nothing
but the motion, water hitting water
hitting stones hitting sticks hitting
my cortex…

◆

Have you ever considered
the structure of a spring
where a whole river can rise
seemingly straight up out of the limestone and go
like a runner at the starting blocks

but it never gets winded
and if the muscles ache
we aren't tuned to hear them.

I tried at 17 to say, *Here, this
is the beginning of my one true life,
0-16 was just a bad start: a rape, a suicide,
the last house we inhabited burnt to the ground…*

I believed then
I could walk away from it.

Now I know a secret.
It has to do with duckweed
decorating the surface of a small lake—
a green gauzy dress
shifting and blowing with every tiny current
like a scene in a movie
that is meant to be poignant
and it is

but not to the snapping turtle
in its darkly textured hood

or the fat grey spider nearly invisible
on the mottled bark of a tree
watching me from two of its eight eyes,
sucking the last juices
out of a brilliant red dragonfly...

◆

When there is a snag or a small whirlpool
I don't want to stop or
dive to fix it:
I want clarity.

I don't want the rough alligator and the smooth log
to resemble each other so strikingly

or the blue heron to rise so simply
like a blue flower
out over the water
making every single reflecting thing
shimmer...

SEAHORSE KEY

There is no other way to explain how we do this:
we census horseshoe crabs, counting
the number of males and females, whether single or
in pairs, noting the percentage of the carapace covered with barnacles
and whether each crab has been previously tagged,
writing all this information on a data sheet
attached to a clipboard
protected from the intermittent rain with plastic
that flaps and gets in the way, using pencils that break easily
in the damp salty air...

Inside the white lighthouse
at the top of the hill
everything is dazzling white,
even in the rain on a cloudy day,
except the wooden floor, painted jade green—
a mere whim of the painters

or meant to simulate grass (there is none on this island).
The effect is surreal, like a Dali painting,
as if there should be hooded or cloaked women
hovering above the horizon.

Instead, we have brown pelicans
nesting in the low trees,
those masters of subliminal grace, preening and squawking
like a crowd of hung-over angels—

no book on the beauty
of the unconventional
would be complete
without a pelican as centrefold—

unless perhaps it contained the astonishing helmets
of the coupling horseshoe crabs, half-buried
in sand or out and about,
swimming in tandem like small railway cars—
ancient, poorly understood, gloomy,
also in peril, also alien, also
in their element, as we stagger to carry them
from water to earth, we who can be tranquil
neither place.

BETWEEN ONE BLUE-GREY ISLAND AND ANOTHER

When it happens—enlightenment, ecstasy,
whatever it's called in whatever language
I am living in by then—
I won't want to come back.

It's like that instant last night
where the lion and I were curled
in each other's arms
and I couldn't tell which was me—
fur or human skin, straw-coloured mane
or short black hair,
having lost all sense of *mine*
and *yours*
having crossed some boundary
that had been holding me inside this body
40 years.

So when it arrives at my balcony
like the wind in my wind chimes,
the chimes I bought in Colorado
to remind me of my childhood,

I will go through the proper rituals and ceremonies,
I will light my dark green candle
and the incense that smells like cinnamon
and the inside of a rain forest,

my ego will get in a small boat
and be benignly abandoned
between one blue-grey island and another.
I'll wave it good-bye sweetly.

I won't miss a thing.

THE WHITE DOOR OF THE MOON

I can't recall the time of day exactly—
when the twilit sky became so much itself
the density of blue
made me dizzy.

Can there be too much beauty? An excess
of joy?

At the same time, from behind the palms,
where it spins fables,
the full moon shimmers a trail
across the water, the kind
you would follow into a dream,
for gravity is of the mind, not the body,

you knock at the white door
of the moon, and open, and enter.

THE EMPIRE OF SNOW

for Ellen Moore and Scott Harrison

The hills look smoked. A fine permanent haze
to which the eyes never adjust.

Icicles along the edge of a small twisting creek.
The water serpentine green or pale blue, moving over ice
or soundlessly beneath it,
over buried leaves, toads estivating in the thick
brown mud, trout slipping beneath the roots
of trees…

Gorgeous yellow snow willows. Rocks
half-buried like a koan. The zen of an avalanche.
A whole hillside of white candles, flickering:
numinous beings in the guise of trees.

The black dog snuffling through deep snow,
following faint trails of rabbit, red fox, mouse,
whiskers iced in a parody of wax-tipped moustache,
all at once shooting up out of drift
into blue light and snow shadows
like a muskrat or otter surfacing.

The tall tawny-coloured grasses,
heads above the drifts, casting mauve shadows
the colour of eyelids.

And in the fields, after the children
have had their energies bundled indoors,
and the late afternoon shadows
seem at a loss,

the asymmetrical snow angels they've made
glow
like the after-image of a large white moth

or a dead baby from the *barrio* in Caracas I saw
dressed as an angel
in a coffin the size of a large man's shoe.

EL AMPARO

When it's dry,
everything flowers.
Small bushes, not listed in any guide.
A twisted tree, blackened as charcoal.
You don't expect to hear hot jazz
blown through the pale orange lips
of the trumpet flowers—but a lament,
slow, half-heard, dirge
of *la epoca seca*.

The fence posts cut last season
have blossomed into two-metre trees,
branches and leaves tossing in the hot morning wind
like a horse trying endlessly to rid itself of flies.
And the poinsettia bracts
scattered here and there across the hills,
how they resemble crimson tailfeathers!

The ripeness of coconuts! Yellow globules, incandescent.
You expect at night
to be guided by their glimmer, warm as candles.
The slick smooth yellow trunks of bamboo.
Countless green textures of leaves.

A few red African tulip blossoms scattered
along the roadside.
Small scarlet pools
like the bodies of the fishermen
murdered in El Amparo.

Shot by members of the army, above the law,
unaccountable.

Lowland tropical forest,
hawks ride the updrafts toward the *Cordillera*,
and far below women wash rainbows in the muddy pools
of a drying riverbed.

Beside them, mustard-yellow flowers,
dense and luxuriant,
weigh down the whole valley with their fragrance.

SAN JUAN BAUTISTA, WITH MAGENTA ANTHURIUMS

The night we arrived in Yaguaraparo, *la reina* was chosen,
at three in the morning, not for her beauty or bearing,
but for her skill in catching and cooking a succulent variety

of land crab, which all the judges had to taste several times
before crowning her with magenta anthuriums. This place
is famous for its hand-painted murals of creatures

from the sea beyond us, and beyond the mangroves
at the ragged edge of town. We catch a whiff
of that stale salty smell, the pungent aftermath

of love-making in a small hotel room with a ceiling fan
which lulls everybody else but me to sleep—
no matter how delicious the idea of self-

perpetuating breeze. Following the newly-crowned queen
down rain-slicked streets, people burst into dance
spontaneously, their bodies supple as serpents.

The statue of San Juan Bautista glows a faint blue
from the light cast by row upon row
of flickering indigo candles.

I wake days later, it seems, alone in a hammock,
in the courtyard of a deserted house. High, lovely
wooden ceilings. Muted green. Pillars someone has kindly attached

my colourful hammock ropes to. Silver streaks of rain
that alternate with the gloomy light filtering
between the slender leaves of mango trees.

The flowers of *Syzygium*, their fuchsia-coloured petals
prodding me languidly awake, and the ripened mangoes,
falling at random onto the rain-soaked, blackened earth.

What It is That's Missing

"And the past, as always, stretched before us,
still, complex, impenetrable."
—Louise Glück

"What I mean is I wanted to live my life
but I didn't want to do what I had to do
to go on, which was: to go back."
—Mary Oliver

LETTER TO MY MOTHER ON THE ANNIVERSARY OF HER SUICIDE

I used to want you to come back into our lives
but now if I saw you hesitating on a streetcorner,
buying fabric at a woolen outlet, slowly raking
autumn leaves or planting the tulip bulbs
that would bloom
red and purple
in the back garden all spring,
I would run as fast as I could
and get a gun,
a silver one inlaid with mahogany and teak,
well-handled, well-oiled, used
by other abandoned children,
and I would hold it at your temple,
where your thick black eyebrows rose and fell
like blackbirds throughout my childhood,
where your lovely white earlobes held
in the glitter of your exotic earrings
all the beauty I had access to,
behind which your anguish
demolished you, and then, without hesitation,
demolished all of us, five children
and a husband, I would level that gun
without a pause, without listening to you
beg for mercy or understanding,
I would stand very straight
and think of the years of obsession,
I would think of the ruin of our lives,
I would pull the trigger
and I would say
this is my life
and I will live it
as far away from your shadow as I can.

WHEN YOU WERE OURS

In the summers at our cottage, the wooden cottage
designed by our father, with huge picture windows
facing the water, and a deck,
and a 30-ft sailboat parked up beneath the house
on a railway flatcar, then
we had you all to ourselves.

Your mother sailed to England as she would do
every summer until her death, and your husband came
from the city only on week-ends.
So you were ours.

These are the only pictures of us I can bear to look at,
even now, so many years later. All of us swimming,
picking raspberries, climbing up into the treehouse,
walking home in the pitch blackness without a flashlight,
finding our way by touch
and the delicate odour of night-blooming flowers,
knowing you were up, waiting, knowing
that huge unspoken love, which was nearly ready to burst,
was waiting, and because you couldn't communicate
feeling, we learned to read you
as a blind person will read scent and sound,
we anticipated your love,
we knew it had to be somewhere,
what mother could have borne these five children
and not loved us
until death do us part.

UNTIL THE RAIN HAS COME AND GONE

Saturday afternoon. There have been
hundreds of them.
A dense green slick feeling
in the air. Thunderclouds building up.
A heaviness that enters
as if through an open door
and will not leave
until the rain has come and gone.

So. Sit on the grey balcony. Listen
to the lonely little creek, singing for no one
but its few fishes and dead yellow leaves.

You cannot have those years back.
You can only go forward into the unknown, the
terrible dark future,
seeking what it is
that's missing.

SHARKS

This morning I was up before dawn
driving to the park at Little Talbot Island
on the east coast of Florida

to contemplate the sea
and cabbage palms and pelicans
and the terns with their black skull caps
and fantastic orange feet

and that terrible sensational roar
of slate grey, burnished green, treacherous blue—
solid glittering mass
pouring down,
being sucked back out
as if into a black hole of the mid-Atlantic galaxy.

Or the sharks, who will notice
my menstrual blood this morning
and from as far away as the Azores

come zeroing in…

Do you realize how much water *weighs?*

Going to crush me like a jelly-fish.

THE DARKER BLUE INSIDE

I keep in my room in Caracas
my mother's olive-coloured vase from China,
the background etched with a repetitive black pattern
like families of snail shells found in a mountain stream
and lined up in rows as a child might do
learning to count
with an abacus.

This is what my mother saw, one of the last things,
and she had been reading that enigmatic book
The French Lieutenant's Woman that must have made her
ache for her life
or for the life she hadn't chosen.

Inserted in front of the wall of snails
is a pink flowering branch—
each flower shaped like a cloud,
each cloud drifting above a gorge,
the gorge suggestive of limitlessness—

and circling the half-moon lid
is a simple design in a shade of turquoise
that isn't quite believable
as, 14 years later, her death still isn't.

My sister used to insist
one day my mother would stroll back into our lives
twirling a parasol
like a vision from a distant century
having been merely lost to us for a while
and now returned as a gift
better than before—

but I take off the lid
and look at the darker blue inside,
the colour of someone's imagined Chinese heaven
full of dragons, monkeys, snakes, wild boars...

What I see is a solitary woman, slumped
on a leather car seat. The leather polished and dark.
One of her hands clenched into a fist.
The other loose, open, in surrender or
supplication.

Inscrutable, her body.
Not yet decomposed.
The hair unmussed. The watch on the wrist
ticking without pause. Silver earrings still warm
from the recent warmth of her body.
The temperature dropping now in the unheated garage.
The snow outside falling and falling.

Her lipstick the colour of tangerines.
A perfect outline of her lips.
As though she had applied it
in the rear-view mirror, clicked shut the tube,
dropped it into her purse, taken out the keys,
turned on the ignition…

How long did she pause?
Did she think of us? Did she remember
her mother, who lived with us all those years,
or her father, who died the same year
her first child was born?

Then she would have started to inhale the gas,
not knowing precisely how long it would take
to feel drowsy, to feel warm…
In her warm coat, fur-lined boots, wearing a scarf,
an ordinary scarf, suffused
with her favourite perfume *Caleche*…

DRIVING, BEING DRIVEN

Driving. Being driven down hairpin curves. Splendid views of green rushing streams and pines and rock faces, gouged by frost and ice and the chaotic history of the surface of the earth. Past glorious stalks of gladioli. Salmon-coloured. Burnt orange. Fuchsia. Straw yellow. Bridal-veil white. With streaming, flickering images at the periphery. With my mother dead fourteen years. Without her hand in my hand, ever. Again. With the anguish of being thirty-eight and nowhere to go. Without enough love. With wraparound green plastic sunglasses. With a pet Amazonian parrot that speaks in dialect. With the latest interpretation of the Maya language near at hand. With skin cells dying off by the hundreds, daily. With the scent of roses impaling me. In my father's garden. With no moon except the fine silver haloing the lettuce leaves. With no lettuce. No roses. Insufficient love. Driving around. In my father's seventeen-year-old rust-coloured Cadillac. No automatic windows, no white leather upholstery. No car. No garden. No father.

OUT OF THE ORDINARY

A letter from my mother was waiting for me
after she died.
It has taken me 10 years
to read it again.

There is nothing
out of the ordinary:
the weather in Colorado in January;
the dusty blue-black of twilight;
in the back yard the same ivory trunks
of the poplars
bordering the garden
that were there in full summer.

Yet it is as though she had painted a picture
and then while I was watching
removed all trace of colour.

Two weeks before she killed herself
she set off on foot to visit her friend
as she had been doing for months, to have a cup of tea…

Her friend opened the door against a driving blizzard
to a woman dressed head to toe in white,
floating like the angel of death
hovering above the doorsill,
a huge mass of calla lilies in her arms.

As if my mother and the angel of death
and the mass of calla lilies
were a single numinous being.

COMPOSITION WITH YELLOW AT THE EPICENTRE

for Phil

In the cathedral of the eucalyptus grove
I hear your mother's 86-year-old voice
quietly identifying some native
California plants: glacier lily, Chinese houses,
footsteps-of-spring, shooting star, coyote mint—

though she has been dead now eight months.
I believe she is back, momentarily,
in the guise of the lemon-coloured fungus
shaped like clouds in Chinese paintings
we discovered in the roots of an overturned
eucalyptus yesterday, above it the entrance

to a wild beehive, a honeycomb in the making
deep in the darkness of the heartwood.

The fungus was cold and delicate as an earlobe
and yellow as the colour of the dead in preconquest Mexico
where food is especially prepared for them
each year on *El Día de los Muertos*

and this fungus, according to an old Amerindian woman,
is delicious, highly edible

so past midnight, sleepless, the air drowsy
with menthol and pine resin, I go to the grove
like a sleepwalker and break off a tiny corner

eating slowly, remembering
the succulent *Dudleya* that surrounds all the borders
of her white wooden house
which every fall sends up orange-red flowers
in the shape of blunt arrowheads
and is called *live-forever*.

THE FLOWER WOMAN AND THE DOG STAR

I'm crying, meandering the broken streets
of Caracas just before dawn, a dangerous time.
A woman in a doorway weaves orange petals of flowers
onto a slender frame.

She begins to tell me her version
of the story of the Dog Star,
where Sirius is so blinded by grief
because his friend the Jaguar has been killed
he cannot see that his own light is fading.
And what would the sailors do, asks the woman,
if the Dog Star extinguished himself?
How would you find your way home?

We both look up instinctively
into the pre-dawn sky, now almost violet.
Behind me is the blackness where I have been lost,
even from myself.
But that is where the Jaguar is.

LONG ISLAND, SUMMER, 1954

I was two years old in 1954
when Norma Jeane sat poised perfectly
on the orange metal bar of a children's
roundabout, the kind that used to make me
dizzy and sick when I spun it out-of-control
faster and faster, hanging from one thin bony arm—
but that was much later, after she was already dead.

Now she wears for the photographer
a striped sleeveless top
the colour of daffodils and black roses,
tiger lilies and the soft pillow-white
of the white narcissus,
holding a copy of James Joyce's *Ulysses*,
showing the whole glorious length of her
flawless legs—burnished, we might say—radiant,
golden, perfect legs. Not a single blemish or scar.

Not for me to say whether or not
she was reading with great attention
because she was in a children's playground in Long Island,
distracted by the photographer, the light,
deep in the middle of her heroic and tragic life,
no end in sight,

and I was in a small provincial town in southeastern Québec
learning to walk, not yet aware
of James Joyce or Marilyn Monroe
or death by suicide.

That was all far off, in the future,
in another country
and I was safe in my mother's arms
as in a fortress of blood, muscle, and singing bone,
a fortress under seige from within,

but this is not apparent in 1954
any more than Norma Jeane's wavering descent
is visible in her calm, sleepy, golden body,
her short bleached blonde hair

or the green shining leaves of the trees
behind her in the park singing,
Light. Light. Light.

BETWEEN TOFINO AND UCLUELET

Whenever I try to describe myself at 18,
living in a small house I built
from plastic, driftwood, rope and nails
on the west coast of Vancouver Island
between the small fishing towns of Tofino and Ucluelet
before it became the Pacific Rim National Park,
people's eyebrows raise slightly,
I sound so, well, *eccentric*.

No clothes. Fasting, sometimes, for days.
Gathering beautiful navy blue mussels
for a feast on the beach one night,
unable to eat them because
they had been so recently, tangibly, *alive*.
Singing a bivalve lament only I could hear.

I wore seaweed braided into my long black hair.
Danced with my shadow on the beach
when the shimmering heat made hallucinations
at the water's edge,
and it was hard not to just plunge in and swim,
maybe forever, drifting on blue waves of light
all the way to China.

There were men, too. Other lost souls.
Wanting things from me I couldn't have given anyone, then.
Men I couldn't bear to touch.

One who licked live ants off his forearms
and ate them, smiling and crunching,
saying, *protein, protein*
like some kind of insane mantra.

And the twin brothers who said the same thing simultaneously
so often we treated them, finally, as a single entity.

A couple whose blonde hair was so long and intertwined
they never went anywhere alone.

I was very thin. Like one long electric nerve ending.
Making starts of conversations
that hung a long time, unanswered, in the dripping air.
Unable to stay through the winter rains. Unable
to stand in any place longer than the blink of an eye
or else paralyzed, in a trance.
Feeding the moon.

Saunas at midnight when we floated away from the earth,
briefly, and languished among the bright mysterious stars
of the Milky Way, hammered into the black night sky
like the shiny relics of long-dead saints.

There was a triangle of immense trees
inland, past the deer meadow and the incandescent
green and orange patches of moss and wild-flowers.
When I sat precisely in the middle
in the warm, motionless, molten afternoons
I was in a force field of living light
I have never experienced since.

One night in a bar I told everything
to somebody I'd never seen before,
and it all got tangled up
with Joanie Baez singing *Diamonds and Rust*
and my failed suicide attempt
and being raped on the highway hitch-hiking
back to Montreal that same year,
the subsequent abortion, nothing
is ever really forgotten, is it.
So we drank more gin and tonic,
and my new friend's stories began to blend right in...

I could have lived there forever.
One rainy day in October
I packed my father's old heavy canvas backpack
and hiked the long muddy trail up among huge silent trees,
pausing at the top where the abandoned radar station
used to be, surveying one last time
the wind pouring in off the sea
like a prayer,
then walking to the island highway
to get to the ferry and the grim rain-slicked streets
of the rest of the world.

WHAT THE LIGHT COULD NOT ERASE

But there are no strangers in dreams...
there are only people in disguise.

—Timothy Findley

I see the impromptu props—rough wood
for the window frames, a bare scarred table,
three men standing, one,
the intended victim,
leaning against the table
as though for balance.

A lamp for which there is no obvious
cord or battery
but this doesn't matter
(it's a dream, remember)
and anyway the light from this blue lamp
penetrates every shadow, every grain
of wood. Very intense. And also
equidistant from everything in the room.

The leaning man—the most ominous
(so it seems when I mull this over
waking, terrified, past midnight)—
is bald with moustache and dark beard.
Burly. Tightly controlled.

There is a scratch at the door,
something to enhance the tension—

and a darkness wells up
that begins to stain the burly man's face.

Which the luminous blue light cannot erase.

I see as the room telescopes
and I fly in through one window
this is the face of the man
who raped me.

As the lamp is smashed,
I pulse through the heavy air,
using echo-location,
avoiding the walls, the
scuffling men.

I can hear
the victim's mind as it slides,
out-of-focus,
down onto the floor
after the body.

And then there are the neighbour's large dogs,
running through the door into the room,
smelling blood and fear,
their golden fur tinged reddish-brown

and I have withdrawn
to become the narrator again
pulled back, watching the men and dogs go at it

but the burly man sits at the table, unharmed.

A DREAM IN SURINAME

Someone, a man in shadows, perhaps the one
who robbed me in Caracas,
shows up at the entranceway
with a pistol.

It is too elaborate, a stage prop,
a dream pistol with genuine ivory handle,
perfect balance, and he is twirling it
like a slightly crazed cowboy in a black western,
parodying himself.

Until he bows to my mother, saying,
Who's first?

There are four daughters. I hold
one sister's hand,
watching my mother shift her weight, willing her
to shout my father's name
but he is gone, him and his Cadillac,
looking for gold in the mountains…

It was settled by a roll of the dice.
I, the eldest, would be first.
He would return at sunset.

I had an erotic fantasy of being tied to a tree,
pistol between my teeth,
while he entered me again and again

and I thought
this must be death
because I was detached from my body,
looking down at this scene
from the black cushion of a thunder-cloud…

I was making the thunder-clouds with my body—
big, dark, threatening ones,
ones that swallow whole villages!

And then my mother touching my forehead
with her cool, steady hand.

TURNING BACK TO THE GREEN

Will you believe me if I tell you
I wasn't—well, not seriously—
abandoned as a child?

And yet I dream of it—being lost, forsaken—
with great frequency.

For example: in Budapest, in a garden terrace,
eating lunch with a group of fellow-travellers.

I notice another garden, an interior one,
in an adjoining building. There's a young woman
airing sheets in a light room,
facing the overgrown, tangled green.

I watch her. She has an arresting face,
like an ikon, suffused with yellow light.

There are black iron stairs,
like fire-escapes, descending
into the flowers.

Flowers that are deep red, their cups
dizzyingly scented.

But I keep turning back
to the green.

It is difficult to leave.
I never speak to the girl, yet
the sense of place exerts some magnetic pull,
charming me.

When I return to the terrace, my companions have left
to catch their plane home
(though it's never clear
where that is), left their lunch
in chaos, left me.

Then I am in Spain.

My car is being repaired by a drunken mechanic.

Most of the engine is in pieces
on a weedy, cracked sidewalk.

I peel oranges, offering him piece after piece.
Anything so he will stop taking out
just one more part.

Then I cannot find my car.

I am standing alone in front of a dark,
shuttered house
where everyone I have ever loved
has lived.

But I am surrounded
by the green.

WOKEN AT NIGHT BY RAIN FALLING

for Andy Brower and Jackie Brown

I slide open my wall-to-wall window
and the hunched shadow of a wood-rat goes by
as though on tiptoe
and something of that shape
or a memory of that shape
enters my dreams
so later I am in a dark labyrinth,
tunnelling for my life

when a storm
bursts across the fields and the small lake,
waking me and drawing me back to the window,
to the night rain
drenching the bent-over lombardy poplars,
the immense ageless oaks, Lebanese cedars, yews,
the intensely red poppies growing wild
at the boundaries of the wheat fields, the grebes
and chiffchaffs, moorhens and mallards,

I want to climb out the window and dance in the field,
I want to stop caring about why I am here,
who I really am, what it is that's missing
or has always been missing.

Beyond Las Nieves

"La Ventolera

Silba el viento dentro de mí.
    Estoy desnudo. Dueño de nada, dueño de nadie, ni siquiera dueño de mis certezas, soy mi cara en el viento, a contraviento, y soy el viento que me golpean la cara."

—Eduardo Galeano

ON THE OTHER SIDE OF LOVE

Ah, my difficult daughter, sighs my mother,
rising one more time from the dead,
an apparition
among the fireflies and incessant violet
flashes of lightning over Casigua,
above the purple flowering *apamate* and palm trees,
above the wood smoke and the smell of oranges
and urine and lime trees…

You're going to burn out
like the orange fire of bucaré blossoms.

I admit I'm consumed by loss—
though I want something larger.
For example, the *Virgen de Coromoto*
could levitate from her new shrine at Guanare
and walk on tiptoe
down the broken blue spine of the *Cordillera*,
flirting with the snow-clouds
gathered over *Pico Bolívar*,
distributing free *lotería* tickets
to every woman and child in Venezuela.

That would cheer me up, at least temporarily.

To have k.d. lang sing *Crying Over You* or
The Yellow Rose of Texas. That would cheer me up too,
except that I live in Florida.

My mother flaps down impatiently, settling
like a semi-precious stone
among the egrets. *I'm getting rather faint*, she says.
And it's true, I can see through her body,
all the way across the Maracaibo Basin,
past the haciendas and saman trees,
the smouldering sugar cane fields, the ponds
mirroring rain clouds and white water lilies:

I dream of making love to another woman
and then the gorgeous head
of a horse-like creature
emerges from the earth
covered with calla lilies and red hibiscus.

There should be a *Virgen del Cebú* here.
What's worshiped is pasture grass
and beef by the kilogram, an occasional rodeo star,
and a man who claims to cure hoof-and-mouth disease
by playing an ancient saxophone beneath a ceiba tree
every afternoon around five o'clock
in the plaza in El Vigía.

What do I want? The satin texture of your skin,
your tongue in my mouth,
your body
curled around mine like a snail.

Make love to me in this hammock, make love to me
on the roof of the *Hotel las Hermanas*,
make love to me among the bruised orange blossoms…

Do you realize I drove all the way from Caracas
in the back of a jeep
with two green parrots
that recited Gabriela Mistral and Cesar Vallejos
in alternating voices
and refused to eat anything but *arepas* and *cambures*?

I'm not looking for delirium or hallucinations.
Something on the other side of love, a parallel
universe, a way out, a way
back in: the gas fires at night lighting
southwestern Zulia, the dark drums of San Benito,
the way the air resonates at noon like a plucked guitar,
the sadness of the mud banks
of the *Río de Oro*.

BLACK IBISES

The blackness is visible and yet it is invisible,
for I see that I cannot see it.

— Jamaica Kincaid

A drowned field. Dozens of black ibises, feeding intently
as though preparing for some stupendous migration.

In the shattered light of mid-day
the broken body of a DC-9
raised on two concrete cradles

overlooks a blue tiled swimming pool surrounded
by barbed wire and jagged glass
embedded in a high stone wall.

Under the plane's belly, a mud-caked jeep.
Windows tinted so dark
there's only the vague outline of a seat-back tilted
against the steering wheel, leaving the impression
of a hurried— perhaps forced— exit.

I am reminded that a foreigner, a biologist,
was kidnapped and beaten recently
in a town not far from this *finca*.

Spotlights on the wings aim at the pool, creating
even in broad daylight
an oasis of blue light.

The owner, a general, spreads his arms
and poses in front of the plane,
wearing sunglasses, holding
a tumbler of scotch.

From one blackened engine, a pink flower
explodes.

Beyond it I can see the purple ankles
of the Andes, which go south almost forever,
through jungles, bivouacs of army ants,
and the spectacular orange plumage of the male
Cock-of-the-Rock.

In a single startled motion, the black ibises rise
above the yellow petals of *Sagittarius*,
above the mute eloquent membrane of water.

There is no real news from this country
without the words *torture*, *violent death*.

HEAVY, SILVER-COLOURED OBJECTS

Phil, Roberto and I take a dirt road through the dense shadows of a palm forest up and then across an old savannah where the earth is mineral red, the long grass glistens. Haphazard boulders, their grey and silver flanks shadowed. The road follows the hill's curve to an abandoned nickel mine. Inside one building, shafts of sun illumine cloudy chemicals in jars. Another building with wooden boxes of drill cores: heavy, silver-coloured.

Wandering alone along the ridge, I realize my father spent most of his life in places like this. Places I imagined for him when he was away and I was growing up without him. In the valley below I can hear fire crackling in the subsoil, the trees covered with orange *bucaré* blossoms, lit-up like Chinese lanterns.

Roberto climbs a tree to collect insects from small bromeliads. In the wild, parched garden Phil watches a slate-coloured bird flit from branch to branch. I catch a glimpse of my father perched on the roof of one of the buildings. He's picking up samples of nickel, glancing at them briefly, and then tossing them casually onto the dry ground. Strewn over the roof at his feet are geological maps - multicoloured, multipatterned: soil types, rock types, outcrops - incredibly detailed. He waves at me vaguely like a president riding in a bullet-proof motorcade, the president of a small island republic on the verge of a *coup*, or, like my father, about to be overwhelmed by his wife's suicide.

BEYOND LAS NIEVES

It's late afternon, the sun's not setting yet,
but you feel in the cooling air how soon it will, and how soon
these trails will get dark, too dark to hike back down

without a flashlight. You have been telling me of a climb
with a fractured ankle in northern Borneo, just because
you had to make it to the top of some peak and I

stop, breathless, as you climb higher and higher.
I am paralyzed by the view of Caracas, so many metres below us,
by the dry smoking hills that surround us completely,

and by the knowledge that we cannot get any closer
to each other than this. Last night in a dream
my bedroom was suffused with a deep peacock blue.

A thick stream of sunlight spilled from a latticed window
and began to move across the Persian rug
like a large sulphur-coloured butterfly.

A wedding party arrived at the door but the man in it
wasn't you, or anyone I recognized.
A young girl handed me flowers— yellow *araguaney*

mixed with orange *bucaré*,
and a set of ornate 19th century keys.
I placed the bouquet

into that stream of sunlight
and it stayed there, in the air, as though I'd put it
on the smooth surface of a lake, water so clear

I could see every detail of the Persian rug
5 metres below. The keys sank immediately,
flashing bronze and silver, twisting.

YOU, NORTH OF ME

A friend once told me that all the women
he'd ever made love to
were part of him,
part of his skin and hair and dreams—
they would never leave
while he was living.

So I think of you, north of me,
north of so many small violent countries,
where some of the night stars are different,
and there's no chorus of tree frogs
lighting up the brief twilight.

How your face looks in the dark.
Your addiction to maps. The way the air
around your arms flickers
as around images of certain medieval saints.
Your sad hands, holding nothing.
My belief that I'll die before you,
and in a plane crash.
Your way of cooking pasta with garlic and hot
chili peppers while listening intently
to Springsteen's *Tunnel of Love*.
The fact that you ignore time
and wear a wristwatch.
Your abandoned skill as a potter.
Your loneliness.
How you once fell asleep on your motorcycle
in a meadow in warm autumn sunlight
and said when you woke it was
the most delicious sleep.

THE SIDE EFFECTS OF MARRIAGE + MALARIA

A postcard arrives from you of Colorado mountains
—I forget which ones—
announcing your impending marriage.

The same day I examine my red blood cells
through a microscope in Caracas
and discover malaria parasites.

This is not cause and effect,
exactly, but like that violent summer thunderstorm
that began the instant my car broke down—

some events don't appear to be random.

The next morning, after a massive dose of chloroquine,
I tried walking up a long hill. Was it grief
that made me lie down
among the fallen purple petals of *Clematis*?

I have never lain down on anything
so soft.

Behind the purple radiance
the spotlights of yellow day lilies
were heating the place up, altogether
too bright.

When I closed my eyes I was lifted, vibrating,
a few centimetres off the earth.

I felt exultant, that I could be free—
and in the next breath
that nothing had changed.

Then the fever and chills began.

THE TIGERS OF PARAMARIBO

are more radiant than Borges' blue dream tigers,
and there are five of them,
indolent, breath-taking,
their carnivorous nature evident
in every stipple of muscle, each stripe and counter-stripe,
as though they themselves were shadow/sun/shadow.

Early morning, hot and muggy, a suburb
on the outskirts of Paramaribo, uncut grass,
nothing alive in the Reptile House,
and one horse slouching its swayback way easily
down the path past the cage, the black bars casting
more shadows, striping the tiger stripes,

and a tall, serious woman, meditating on
tigerness,
unable to get past the first swallow of raw antelope,
sketches, takes detailed notes...

Then the tigers, all five at once, crouch
belly-flat, ears down,
and rush *en masse* as though on cue
at the horse.
They leap up, seemingly bending the bars,
fall back, leap again

and the man with the camera runs toward the woman,
thinking the tigers have been provoked
by her black-and-white zebra leggings
(he hasn't seen the horse)

but she has now managed
to swallow the whole antelope
and slipped between the bars, calmly
looking out at him, licking her massive
paws.

A FIELD, A LILY, A GREAT WHITE EGRET

Let us say the lily in this inundated field
becomes a splendidly carved object made of onyx
placed with great care on a dark wooden pedestal
like a sculpture of a woman reclining
on one elbow, head in profile,

with a great white egret motionless,
in the foreground,
not far from her feet.

But, let us say that the egret remains an egret.
That way, when it finishes fishing
in the glazed afternoon light, it can fly away.

Meanwhile, the lily is pulsing, shimmering—
the way the inside of a freshly-baked loaf of bread
appears to a woman or a man after some months
in solitary confinement: not real.

Later, past nightfall, the egret is gone.
Asleep in the branch of a tree, out of sight.
The lily glows in the half-light of the half-moon,
its petals extended
like a multi-armed Hindu goddess
simultaneously offering joy, pleasure, despair and death.

People begin to arrive slowly, as though sleep-walking,
drawn by the light. Until dawn, they murmur
near the lily in hushed reverent voices.

Sunrise a batik. The lily discreetly transforms itself
into a shadow, following the egret
out of the picture.
This leaves a few people, looking suddenly frightened,
abandoned. Then they leave too.

THE SKY OVER THE SENO DE RELONCAVI

From a dream of making love
to a beautiful, delicate *notro* tree in bloom
I awake
tangled among the pillows and sheets
in a cool hotel room in Puerto Montt.

Out the window, the heavy sky
lights up as if from the glow of a hidden votive candle.

Into the dove-grey stillness
comes a man, standing on a wooden cart full of milk cans,
urging two dappled horses on,
driving them down the middle of the *avenida*
stopping here and there,
telling each customer
someone's child drowned during the night.

The white fragments of shells
that line the walkway along the waterfront
are bits of the moon
that fell while the elderly couple
whose adopted son this was
waited and prayed

and when they emerged, grey-faced
in the morning air, they were shrunken
nearly beyond recognition.

Very slowly, arm in arm they walk
to the water's edge
but the ocean, vast and indifferent
and roiling after last night's storm,

is sullen, and will not comfort them.
And the wind, which before dawn shifted to the north,
speaks only of the end of summer, scattering
the crimson *notro* blossoms
everywhere among the broken shells.

BETWEEN THE GOLFO DE ANCUD
AND THE GOLFO CORCOVADO

lies the town of Castro, near the head of a fjord,
dominated by the gaudy orange
Iglesia de San Francisco
constructed of corrugated metal
by the Italian Eduardo Provosoli in 1906.

The interior gives the sensation
of being inside the wooden hull of a very large ship—
and the light—I wanted to tell you
how the air rippled as the light pulsed through it
like a school of tropical fish.

Light the colour of rye or straw.
Transubstantiated. Transubstantiating
the wooden walls and ceilings and saints
and the old woman who sold me a postcard
of the church, photographed at night, the sky
behind the twin orange and purple towers
so pregnant with pre-storm forebodings

when I walked out onto the steps, later,
into the mid-day sunlight, dazed by the contrast,
I thought the sepia-toned pelicans
circling the fishing boats
in the harbour
were reincarnated angels.

Weren't they?

THE SILVER-STUDDED LIGHT

Another way to see the Strait is to take a taxi
up the muddy, rutted hill to *Cerro Mirador*,
the only place in the world
where one can ski
overlooking the dense aquamarine and silver
skin of the sea
and consider the voyage of Hernando de Magallanes
in 1520, the first foreigner to navigate
the South American Atlantic coast
and make it through the treacherous and stormy
estrecho, searching for a passageway
to the *islas Molucas*.

What he found was
the Pacific.
What he found was the beginning of the end
of 4 indigenous peoples: Aonikenk, Selknam,
Yámanas, and Kaweskar.

After checking out the view through binoculars,
a young Frenchman and I sit inside
with the noisy downhill skiers,
trading stories over the tangerine coals
of a wood-fire.

Coming back down we let the cars and the last bus
go by because
we have much to tell each other,
striding downhill
toward the ocean,

with the indigo of late afternoon snow shadows
and the southern lap-wings
quivering like black and ivory boomerangs
in the silver-studded light
that hangs over Tierra del Fuego,
the end of the world.

THE END OF CHILEAN WINTER

for Pedro Emilio Hernández

Because it is off-season, the end of Chilean winter,
I am the only one walking,
tramping the muddy pathway in the
Reserva Forestal Autoctona
where the rows of *raulí* and *canelo* give way gradually
to a few immense *ulmo* trees

and then up through the yellow spray of bamboo
to a wooden bench with a view
of Volcán Osorno, the top obscured by clouds
clotting around it like cream.

On the way out I pause at the green shutter
of a farmhouse window
as a woman explains the botanical research
and her young black-haired son
brings me tea in a blue painted bowl.

Small bushes outside her window blush
with pale pink flowers.

The unruffled blue of Lago Llanquihue
smooth as the mass graveyard
recently discovered at Biobío

and the photojournalists' exhibit
in Santiago
of the brutal suppression of the resistance
to Pinochet's regime—

a young woman under the eyes
of young soldiers with machine guns
protecting the photographs,
calmly and deliberately coloured in
with red lipstick all the blood
on the revealing black and whites—
lipstick the same colour
as the banners waving in the streets

and all the roses
thrown toward Salvador Allende's coffin—
displayed in glass
on top of a black limosine driving 70 kph
from Viña-del-Mar to Santiago.

At such a speed nothing could touch it.

THE BIGGEST SPECIES OF HYLID FROG IN BARINAS
JOINS US FOR DINNER

We were eating dinner at El Parral—
no, that's not accurate. We had ordered
dinner, drinking ice-cold *cerveza*
with fresh limes—
Jorge and Ramon quietly hung-over and subdued
quietly sipping sweet melon juice.

Minute beetles and leafhoppers skimmed
the surface of the drinks, hobnobbing
with the lime skins.
As the *salsa* poured its monotonous beat
out of the jukebox,
a young girl began to dance by herself
in the centre of the room.

With a spectacular leap, a huge hylid frog
landed in the middle of the dance floor.
The girl crowed at it gleefully, *Dance with me,*
Señor rana, dance
with me.

But it just sat gazing at the lights,
its padded feet glistening,
its dark mottled skin
glowing like radium.

MARGARITA'S STORY

In her sunken garden, the strangler fig
cracks the pot and lifts muscled branches
up through the black grille. In the *llanos*
it would be smothering a palm.

So when a Venezuelan friend refers to an entwined couple
as a *matapalo*, I can feel the man
taking all the available light
from his lover, his chlorophyll molecules
pulsing and trembling to grow, grow!

The ceramic wind chimes attached to the fig
twirl very slowly
back and forth, making not a sound.
Yet watching them one is mildly expectant,
a little irritated at the dull silence.

Then it's evening and the tiny frogs hop up
out of the watery cups of the bromeliads.
They love the dark
upright piano Margarita plays every evening
and when the piano tuner comes once a month
to manipulate the hammers and strings and small screws
that come undone in the moist air

the frogs, perhaps imagining him to be
an odd species of their own kind,
begin to sing like a Greek chorus,
lamenting some amphibian tragedy
louder and louder
until he trembles, telling them to shut up
he has work to do
but they don't shut up.
They're going to sing all night.

THE WOODEN DOORS OF COCHABAMBA

Cochabamba! Not to see again
your hundred wooden doors, ragged
dust-filled trees, not to eat small stale sweet cakes
for breakfast accompanied by even sweeter
coffee. Not to spend an afternoon
at the textile market, exchanging
my wooden zebra bracelet for a pair of earrings, buying
orange and gold and purple woven cloth,
and expounding mournfully
on the destructive influence
of Northamerican greed & waste & provinciality.
Not to be asked why Bolivian scientists
cannot get funded to study the grazing behaviour
of Canada geese. Not to watch a daylong parade
in which the bystanders
are surreptitiously watching us
watch them. Not to find a book
by a Japanese-Bolivian poet
who grew up in the small Amazonian town
we are flying to the next day.
Not to be the only *extranjeras*
attending a satirical play
in which *el diablo* and *tío Sam*
manipulate a *campesino* to take his land
in a manner simultaneously
stereotypic and true-to-life.
Not to enter those wooden doors, and stay.

VILLA TUNARI

Lying in a strange bed,
turquoise sheet twisted around restless,
twisting legs.
Sick with the aftermath of food poisoning,
Salmonella from last night's egg *tortilla*
or something more virulent
in the *salsa picante*.
The acute throbbing behind the eyes, thirst
that has no cure.

Closing my eyes at 5 pm, knowing
"rest" and "sleep" are prescribed,
unable to stop or even slow down the manic bursts of thought.

Listen, then.

The call of the oropendula, nesting high
in the royal palm, how she sounds
like a melancholy stream, rippling.
From the banks of the *Río Tunari,*
the unmistakable raucous *guacamayo,*
splendidly attired in saffron and indigo,
fussing and demanding attention
like a small general
in his labyrinth.
And behind their calls, other birds, but fainter,
unidentifiable.

Drift off into waking sleep, barely conscious.

Rain on the red tile roof. Termites,
chewing their way from Cochabamba to Senegal.
Earthworms, unattractive by any standards,
burrowing beneath the floor.
The rumble of logging trucks, weighed down
with the thoughts (ours, not theirs) of the demise
of the rainforests.

By 8 PM when I'm fully awake again,
lonely, a little wistful,
the oropendula are silent, swaying
in their nests, listening to the wind
telling secrets to the palm leaves.

Couldn't we become their feathered bodies,
olive-green,
trimmed with chesnut and bright yellow?

Colours repeated by tree frogs whose clamour
replaces the birdsong, the rattle
and rasp of insects,
and the odd creaking of roof tiles
as though rodents were celebrating their possession,
once again (now that the humans are distracted,
eating, or otherwise engaged),
of the night.

AMAZONIAN RAIN

for Maria Goreti Rosa-Freitas and Alex Sibajev

Driving the hard-packed red dust road,
sun tormenting the idea
of the back of the neck
(listen to the skin cells whine),
hot wind and dust and a new kind of human desert—
the Amazonian Basin, the frontier,
thousands of hectares of exquisite
flora and fauna—

except a lot of it has already been "disappeared"—
less than the bones remain of the forest,
who's going to remember
what a rosewood *seed* looked like?

So here are the famous moon-white *cebú* cattle
grazing the poor-quality imported grass for a few years,
spawned from fires and bulldozers and wealthy ranchers
and their hired gunmen
and the extermination of local tribes and the murder
of Chico Mendes...

But there was a whole
interconnected world here, intricate and complex,
animals, plants and humans
—and on all of them equally
fell the green Amazonian rain

which we can see coming as fast as the wind toward us,
the whole thing bearing down
as the first drops
let loose on the dead boa constrictor by the roadside
and the noisy parrots
clustered like feather dusters in the fruit trees
and the lone Brazil-nut tree

rising like a tidal wave
above the grove of rubber trees
and our upturned faces
opening like flowers...

Wash away the red dust,
the heat, the useless grandiose
Amazonian dreams. For which, like gold fever,
there is no cure.

Love as a Moving Object

"De dónde viene? they said.
De Tejas.
Tejas, they said. Y dónde va?
He drew on his cigarette. He looked at their faces.
One of them older than the rest nodded at his cheap
new clothes.
El va a ver a su novia, he said."

—Cormac McCarthy

THE DOOR THE ANHINGAS KEEP OPEN

Just where Manatee Springs
empty their bubbling, aquamarine water
into the Suwannee's black,
in the dense morning mist,
in an oak tree laden with
the pale green feathers of Spanish moss,
the anhingas were creaking open
the black hinges of their wings.

Look inside. You will find
the high, uneasy plateau of middle age,
where everyone who isn't contemplating divorce
is undergoing some kind of metamorphosis,
the body urging,
This is it!
Last chance to change everything!

But other anhingas are fishing—
their heads popping up above the water surface
into the little clouds of mist
like surprised champagne corks

and two white herons
and their white-suited visitors
open their ivory fans
and then snap them shut
like someone shuffling a deck of cards.

Don't tell me what is or isn't possible.

I'm busy stalking a slate-blue heron
that is busy stalking a wiggling silver streak
of pure protein.

I know that fish led an exemplary life,
had a mother and father and cousins—but look,
there's no such thing in life as *fair*.

Besides, that fish descended from a long line
of famous *literati*—
one the subject of an ode by Pablo Neruda,
another immortalized on the cover
of Carol Shields' *The Orange Fish*...

Can you see it?
up above the tea-coloured stumps of cedar,
there goes
the fish-inside-the-heron,
turning into flight muscles, into
the heron's eye.

WHITE LILIES, PROVINCETOWN

I cannot free myself of the oversize white lilies
I saw today in Provincetown—
top heavy, spilling their loveliness
petal by petal
onto the greedy overbright grass…

I was one of them!
Unable to move, paralyzed by longing…

as though what hadn't fallen—
stamens and pistils—the apparatus of sex,
was as exposed as my feelings are for you.

Do you see I am terrified?
As if one small touch could…

A TINY GLIMPSE INTO THE FUTURE

Hearing your voice on the answering machine
for the first time
shocked me. Why
was that? To hear my name,
then yours,
in the same breath.

Is it foolish
to imagine oneself in love
in one's fortieth year?

I think there is too much history between us—
all the others who have come before...
And yet—

It is winter, or what passes for winter
in the south. A few leaves drift down.
The sky is pewter.

The raccoon tracks in the mud of the creek
behind my house
like cuneiform, some message
I cannot decipher.

And when I see the moon, it is like
a tiny glimpse into the future:
a stream of light
into which one may accidentally
stray, coming home alone,
finding your voice.

NOTHING PREPARES YOU FOR YOUR OWN DEATH

As I cycled west past the theatre
I was riding for my life
toward the conflagration
masquerading as sunset
which lit-up the southern pines
and casuarina

but at the same time, over the mute grey pyramid
at the museum
the slimmest sliver of moon—
exactly like the curve
of an eggshell—
was, shyly, beginning
to let itself be seen.

Nothing prepares you for your own death.
The little aches and pains,
the time it takes, now,
to heal a torn ligament, say,
in the elbow,
that incapacitates you for *months*.

And the runners I used to be able to pass,
all those muscled, driven
bodies, they were going in the same direction
I was, into the fire.

THE URGE TO START A NEW RELIGION

There are days, many of them, lately,
when I almost understand the urge
to start a new religion,
when my room fills slowly with spirits
like a damp hallway with spilled perfumes—

or perhaps it was that day in November
when my shadow seemed longer than usual
and I discovered
I had absentmindedly taken on the shadows
of several dead friends and relatives:

a poet, an ex-lover, two grandmothers,
my mother, a road-kill raccoon, an ancient
rattle-snake...

Poor shadows! They were bereft,
bodiless,
and I was so lonely...

Anyway, nothing really *dies*, that's a universal
law.

When I look up at the hard relentless stars
on long sleepless nights,
I salute them,
me and my shadows.

IMMORTALITY & CO.

Awake at two in the morning
out of some odd episode about a gila monster,
its orange and black stripes
no doubt making me think
about tigers (my favourite carnivores)

or maybe it was that reptilian sensuality
arousing me—I'd prefer to caress a snake
than some (ahem) men—

Anyway the gila monster was deep in conversation
with a century plant—they were discussing
immortality and Kafka...

It was a desert (of course), searing sunlight,
no oasis in sight, the century plant melancholy
(not due to flower for 25 years), wanting to know

What was the point of it all, anyway.
: Ottmar Liebart's *Nouveau Flamenco.*
Gertrude Stein in Paris. Eduardo Galeano.
Woody Allen's latest film.
Self-Portrait with Braid, 1941 by Frida Kahlo

on my bedroom wall, the necklace of dark grey skulls,
totemic faces & stones—which is what really
woke me up. The braids pulsating.
Ugly, pointed leaves in place of a dress,
the stem winding its way about her hair. Death

definitely on the agenda.
Seductive death—
not a metaphor for anything.

BLACK-HEADED BUDDHIST GULLS, WITH HURRICANE

I do not know
if I will ever be peaceful again.
I don't know what to do
about the constant agitation
that is everywhere I look
in the world.

Today, on Padre island, far up the beach,
to the north, at the intersection
of sky and sand and ocean,
there was a haze
like a hurricane's black heart,
pulsating, sucking the images around it in
like some huge machine gone awry.

It was so violently alive! Not wasting a single second
of its chaotic, windy life.

In the face of it, three black-headed Buddhist gulls
watched young sanderlings
peck fruitlessly at dense masses of opaque, frilly flesh—
jellyfish strewn along the sand
like abandoned parasols.

The gulls did nothing, hunching further down
into the warm, beaten-gold sand.

My lover and I ran and ran,
into the midst of it, against all common sense,
wildly joyful, exhilerated, our mood barometric…

At one point I shouted and screamed
but there was only the roar of the air, vibrant
and taut as a harp string.

When it stopped abruptly, there was a sense,
just for an instant,
of our bodies racing along the shoreline
without us. As though a grand amnesia
had taken hold of us— we didn't care,
we were amoebae, or octopi,
or eel grass, our minds gone out into the Gulf
with the storm, to be returned whimsically,
polished and licked clean
as driftwood.

FIN-DE-SIECLE BLUES, CORPUS CHRISTI

Over the doorway to the Mexican restaurant,
painted fish—gaudy pink, bold yellow, turquoise—
and then inside
clouds
on the ceiling, a triumverate of fish
in every corner, neon strips of dark blue and green,
the sound of bubbling water
and I found myself struggling just to breathe.

Once I passed through here with an old lover,
I was a depressive, it was
another life.

The *fin-de-siècle* blues.

Restless from the hot green Gulf winds
threatening hurricanes, daily,
unable to sleep, anywhere,
we drank a bottle of Mezcal and made a pact
to jump off a pier, seduced by the ocean,
its largesse, its majestic *presence*,
forgetting about tides, forgetting one of us
couldn't swim.

There was no moon, it was overcast, I was
obsessed with this man. There must have been sharks,
waiting. Poisonous jelly-fish, barracuda, electric eels!
After all, this was the Gulf of Mexico.

I never understood what he wanted,
except that it wasn't me.

Since there was no other way out, I jumped.

THE FIFTH INHABITANT OF MEXICO

for Jan Washburn

Emmylou Harris' blues
and Lyle Lovett's lyrics ricochet
around my room like firecrackers at a funeral.

Except that it's 4 am and a red-eyed tree frog
is going to leap off the wall
into my fizzing grapefruit drink,
maybe swim around awhile,
maybe lip synch Lyle Lovett.

After all, the frog is looking decidedly sexy
in its green body suit, and me,
well, I'm kind of lonely,
a pushover for any amphibian, especially one
speaking fluent Spanish
from the rain forests of Costa Rica.

In the background of Frida Kahlo's
Four Inhabitants of Mexico,
hidden in the adobe houses and church,
in the damp shade, in the crevices,
were Mexican frogs—green ones, poisonous ones,
ones that fit into the stunning speckled
mouth of an orchid, glass ones, ones with
red toes...

Hidden because they could see into the future
(Frida painted this picture in 1938),
the future
where they would become one of the mysterious
disappearing acts of the late twentieth century...

Amphibians are the Crown of the Evolutionary Tree!

If I ever get to heaven I'm not going in
unless the frogs are there first.

HOW TO THINK ABOUT SOUTHERN CALIFORNIA

I

I fly alone across the continent—no strings attached.
From the dull green hurricanes of Florida
over the midwest and its dreams of corn,
over the Grand Canyon and the white
vertebrae of snow-capped mountains.

To get to the Pacific
to think about you. And I do, but not in any way
you might imagine.

(Whatever you might feel, this is not
a love poem).

II

I know. I know. Eucalyptus trees
are no longer politically or environmentally
correct because they're non-indigenous (like us),
displace native oaks, grow as fast
as bamboo. But they transform these sere landscapes
into mentholated heaven! And their cutlass-shaped
leaves cut the dry desert wind
into dusty green ribbons of light.

Have you seen how the monarchs,
hundreds of them, cluster among the eucalyptus,
opening and closing their orange and black fans,
making whole groves levitate?

III

We had been walking for hours among creosotebush,
ocotillo, and cholla cactus. The light was
merciless, stunning. We had climbed huge granite boulders
and slithered back down them, finding hidden
blossoms in crevasses, galls and scale insects
on every leaf and branch. It was mid-afternoon
and we were dehydrated, almost delirious.

Jocelyn saw the cattails first, then we all saw
the yellow willows, and the water—
shimmering, dark mineral blue—
and a flock of mallards, serenely paddling around
like theosophists.

One of the many delusions of the desert.

IV

These days I want only to emulate
the yucca night lizard
that lives its whole life
under the bark of a Joshua tree,
emerging at dusk, when the moon is full…

I am learning to love the tarantula, the
sidewinder, and the long-legged kangaroo rat.
To preserve water in any form. To think of you
as an oasis I may only sip at
when in dire need.

Tell me everything you know
about the habits of the small burrowing owl,
the one Jesse James tamed and kept
on his shoulder to ward off bullets
and the evil eye.

In this landscape everything
is stripped away. It is where the cult of peyote
and the secrets of medicine women and men begin.
The light is confrontational. There is nowhere to hide
from yourself.

THE WOMAN'S FACE ALWAYS PRESSED
AGAINST THE WINDOW

This is how I live now.
Looking in on my life like a guest at a party.
Eating ginger snaps and drinking ice-cold
lemonade. Sitting on a balcony of stars.

Sometimes the moon sends me messages
through my giant fern. We commune.

I think of all the useless conversations I have been in,
feeling ethereal as smoke. Transparent.
Breaking down into the component parts.
Here a hand, there an ear, here a heart.
You can bury the hand in the mine in Asbestos,
the heart in Punta Arenas, and, as for the ear,
just throw it to the sharks off the east coast of Florida.
After all, I have been feeding on my fear of them for years.

When I lived in Caracas I watched movies every night,
mesmerized by melodrama and make-up. Thinking how many
locks were between me and the darkness.
Because I couldn't feel, I examined objects
and described them in notebooks in obsessive detail.
I recall an orchid, for example, that went on for days.
I stuck glow-in-the-dark stars on the ceiling
and invented new constellations every night
to the sound of gunfire from the *barrios*
that surrounded the house.
Always a feeling of bravado and desperation
in the pollen-filled air I inhaled every minute
like an asthmatic.

THE SEDUCTIVENESS OF SADNESS

How seductive sadness is.
How like a relationship going sour,
say, like milk, left out by accident
one hot muggy night,
when you and your lover are stoned
and have had too much good white wine,
absorbed, intensely but temporarily,
by each other's skin, and he leaves, saying
this isn't what he wants, and you fall asleep,
still stoned, and that's it.
Spoiled. Irretrievable.

Love, like certain chemical reactions,
has a way of going in one direction only.

Oh you line of least resistance,
you said to him once.
He left soon afterward.

Perhaps you hadn't wanted him to stay, anyway.

Who can read the contradictions
in a late-night phone call from your ex-husband
who's slightly drunk, but somehow sweet
and sort of endearing,

who says, *I just wanted you to know...*
and the rest is lost in the background blur
of the bar music
cranked up really loudly
as though the sound could fill
all the emptiness in the corners of our psyches.

You think a long time about calling him back.

LOVE AS A MOVING OBJECT

Listening to Kate Bush on the slow
early morning drive to work
past the huge oaks and bright pink houses on 6th Street,
past a disgruntled man in black leather
pushing his dysfunctional Harley along the sidewalk,
it's going to be at least 90° in the shade,
and Kate is singing in her passionate, articulate way
about being in love
and never getting out of it...

We all know what that means.
It means to be stalled, trapped,
stuck—because love is a moving object,
like a duck to a duck hunter
who wakes up at 3 am and dresses
in prickly long underwear and hip waders,
shivers in the pre-dawn light, the clouds
racing, scattered and eerie overhead,
who gets cramps in his legs, who needs
desperately to sneeze, who strains to see
that fine line dividing water from air,
he listens acutely for their telltale calls,
keeps concentrating *out there*,
focused on the weather, the ducks' weather,
he is like a man
who is very attendant to women,
who gives the illusion of intimacy
without the intimacy,
the way the duck hunter takes such good care
of his beautiful hand-painted decoys
and guns,
the way he savours every sweet mouthful
of roast duck, later, after he has carried
the handfuls of warm dead bodies
by the necks and flung them
into the back of his pick-up truck
and called it a day.

MEDITATION ON LOSS AND THE COLOUR RED

Every night during that long hot Florida summer
I came home from the gym
or the movies or dinner with a new friend
and I looked at photographs of all my ex-lovers,
and my parents at a mining convention in South Africa
in 1952, the year of my birth, my mother
in flawless white leather gloves and pearls,
my father grinning and elusive,
and myself at 23, a few weeks after my mother's suicide—
smoking a Cuban cigar, a scarf knotted carelessly
at my throat, a silver ring from Mexico on my right hand…

The ex-lovers I shrug off like too-small garments,
I send them to be recycled, I say,
there was no future.
For my mother I build an elaborate wooden reliquary,
which I might burn, someday. Everything
within and without is red.
Paris is Burning and nobody noticed.
Nobody noticed blood
and the mysterious disappearance
of beefsteak tomatoes from American grocery stores.
Nobody noticed inflamed and bloodshot eyes
after too much dope or too much
weeping and wearing a lipstick called *Eat Your Heart Out*.
It doesn't snow in north-central Florida
and I'm homesick for Montreal and I never saw her dead.
There is a blown-up black-and-white of my youngest sister,
age three, sitting beside her best friend Barbara,
pinned up on my fridge so I see it every am
when I take my multiple vitamins
and it gives me a terrible unfinished feeling.
Nothing else smells like a wild red rose
hidden among the blackberry bushes on the west coast

of Vancouver Island on a hot day in July. She was
furious, depressed. We didn't have a funeral.
I don't know how to dream
in the language of mothers. I'm not a mother. I'm not
my mother.

THE MAN WITH MY MOTHER'S HANDS

is here again, at the door, greeting me,
I want to buy a brand-new used car, and he has
a whole basement full of them.
Every colour you can imagine! Magenta,
lemon-yellow, creamy white, the colour of violets,
of bluebird eggs, malachite, sandstone!

But first I must pass through the garden labyrinth
without getting lost. He takes my hand,
but his hand is my mother's hand, with coral
nailpolish on long tapered nails, and this hand
has a will of its own. Soon I am flying
over the garden, looking down at its intricate paths,
dead-ends of poison oak and brambles, the circular trails
through scarlet poppies and drowsiness, the stinging
nettles in amongst the roses...

And then I go down into the basement
where there's a white piano in one corner
on which I must somehow play a brilliant composition
which I cannot do
but then my mother's hands descend
down the stairs behind me and begin to skim
across the notes, two wild swallows
making sounds like the wind dancing with leaves in autumn
or the stars humming during daylight, when they think
no one can hear them

and I am nearly ready to see the cars

but a young girl wearing red felt shorts
with real stars sewn into them
looks up from her drawing
and asks me about the goblin
in the next room beneath the coffee table.

The goblin is black and formless and she is not afraid of it
but I am terrified. My mother's hands rush in
but they are swallowed up. The car salesman follows.
The girl and I sit down near the goblin
and begin to tell it a story...

Glossary

apamate (Tabebuia rosea) — native to Latin America, this tree produces an abundance of light pink flowers

arepas — typical Venezuelan food item, a small thick round bread made of corn flour and usually stuffed with seafood, cheese, avocado or meat and eaten with obligatory *salsa picante*

araguaney (Tabebuia chrysantha) — Venezuelan national tree which blossoms during the dry season with intense yellow flowers

barrios — slums, usually found around large cities

bucaré (Erythrina poeppigiana) — a native of northern South America, this large lovely tree with striking orange flowers has often been used historically to shade young coffee trees in coffee plantations

cambur —- small extremely sweet local banana, never exported

canelo (Drimys winteri) — a beautiful white flowering tree sacred to the indigenous Chilean *Mapuches*

estrecho — strait

finca — ranch or farm

guacamayo — large blue and yellow macaw, *Ara ararauna*, very noisy call, often found in flocks up to 25 in number

llanos — region of west-central Venezuela, very flat and savannah-like, characterized by dry tropical forest with marked seasonality (dry/wet)

matapalo — palm and strangler fig commonly seen growing together in the *llanos*. The parasitic fig eventually kills the palm, though they may grow together for years.

notro (Embothrium coccineum) — tall attractive tree with bright red flowers, native to southern Chile

oropendula (Gymnostinops yuracares) — large attractive bird that lives in colonies; nests are long, pendulous, often suspended from the end of branches

rana — frog

raulí (Nothofagus alpina) — a deciduous thick-barked tree, indigenous to central Chile

Sagittarius — aquatic plant with attractive yellow flowers

Syzygium malaccense — originally from the Malayan archipelago with brilliant pink needle-like stamens and petals

ulmo (Eucryphia cordifolia) — large majestic trees, especially common around Valdivia in central Chile

Notes

Translation by Jan Conn of p.9 by Cristina Peri Rossi

The light of poetry was extinguished by a cloud overloaded with administrators. All of them burned up in the same explosion, ending the age of innocence, leaving only slow, solitary fish, the tooth of an aviator, and three literary chroniclers. These write to the wind.

Translation by Cedric Belfrage of p.55 by Eduardo Galeano

THE GUST

The wind whistles within me.

I am naked. Master of nothing, master of no one, not even master of my own convictions, I am my face in the wind, against the wind, and I am the wind that strikes my face.